```
J              6045702
599.74         15.95
Mar
Markert
Polar bears
```

DATE DUE			
AP 10 '95			
MY 29 '95			
JY 17 '95			
AG 16 '95			
SE 18 '95			

Ry

GREAT RIVER REGIONAL LIBRARY

St. Cloud, Minnesota 56301

GAYLORD M2G

POLAR BEARS

POLAR BEARS

JENNY MARKERT

THE CHILD'S WORLD

DESIGN
Bill Foster of Albarella & Associates, Inc.

PHOTO CREDITS
Jim Brandenburg: 2, 8
Thomas D. Mangelsen/Images of Nature: front cover,
back cover, 10, 13, 17, 19, 21, 23, 31
Tom and Pat Leeson: 6
Joe McDonald: 26, 29
W. Perry Conway: 15
Joe Van Os: 25

Text copyright © 1991 by The Child's World, Inc.
All rights reserved. No part of this book may be
reproduced or utilized in any form or by any means
without written permission from the Publisher.
Printed in the United States of America.

Distributed to schools and libraries
in the United States by
ENCYCLOPAEDIA BRITANNICA EDUCATIONAL CORP
310 South Michigan Ave.
Chicago, Illinois 60604

Library of Congress Cataloging-in-Publication Data
Markert, Jenny.
 Polar bears/Jenny Markert.
  p. cm. — (Child's World Wildlife Library)
 Summary: Describes the physical characteristics, behavior,
 and habitat of the polar bear.
  ISBN 0-89565-708-2
 1. Polar bear — Juvenile literature. [1. Polar bear. 2. Bears.]
 I. Title.
 II. Series.   91-13468
QL737.C27M34 1991   CIP
599.74'446—dc20   AC

Dedicated to all the students at Sacred Heart School

The mighty polar bear is the main attraction at many public zoos, and rightfully so. These cuddly looking, furry white animals are one of the biggest bears in the world. They can grow up to nine feet tall and can weigh nearly as much as a small car. However, cages made of concrete and wire are not the polar bear's natural home.

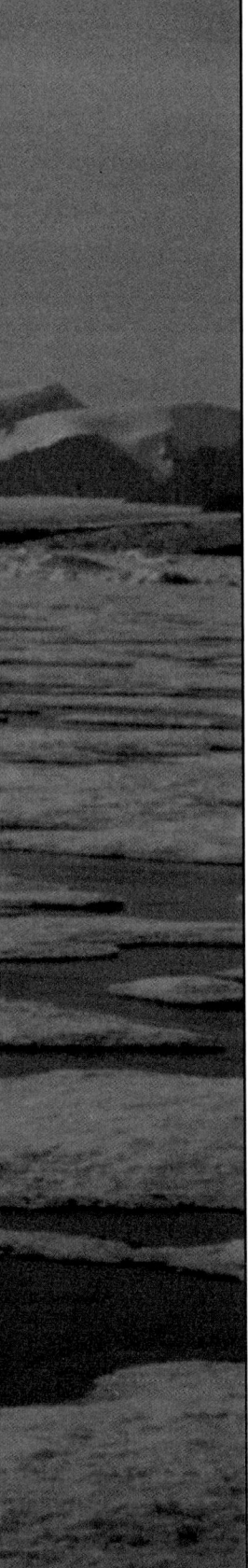

Wild polar bears live in the Arctic, near the North Pole. The Arctic is mostly ocean, surrounded by North America, Asia, and Europe. The Arctic is one of the coldest places in the world. In the winter, the temperature is always far below freezing, and the ground is covered by snow and ice. Most of the ocean is frozen all year round, even in the summer!

The Arctic is too cold for the likes of most human beings. However, polar bears are well equipped for this cold, frozen world. Beneath their skin, polar bears have a thick layer of fat called *blubber*. It keeps them warm, even when they swim in the cold ocean water. The blubber also keeps the bears from starving when food is hard to find. They use it as a food reserve.

Polar bears also have thick fur coats that help to keep them warm. Polar bears are one of the furriest animals on earth. They even have fur on the soles of their feet! This fur keeps their paws warm during long journeys on the ice and snow. It also prevents the bears from slipping on the icy ground. The polar bears' furry feet muffle the sound of their footsteps, too. These big animals walk very quietly.

Polar bears spend most of their lives in and around the Arctic Ocean. They are great swimmers and divers. Some people have seen polar bears swimming 200 miles from land! Adult polar bears can swim five miles per hour. That's faster than you can walk!

When they swim, polar bears close their ears and noses to keep the water out. They swim like dogs, paddling with their big front paws. Their back legs hang down in the water and help them steer.

Polar bears find their food in the water. They eat crabs, fish, and seabirds. They also like bigger sea animals such as porpoises, walruses, sharks, and whales. However, seals are their favorite food.

Polar bears spend most of their time hunting. They usually eat and hunt alone. Polar bears use many tricks to capture their prey. They sneak up on animals that relax in the sun. Polar bears also wait patiently by holes in the ice. Seals pop their heads through these holes in order to breathe. Polar bears have powerful legs and long, sharp claws to help them hook their prey.

Polar bears cannot talk like human beings can. However, they still communicate. They use body language and their voices. They become upset if they cannot catch anything for dinner. They may roar and kick up a cloud of snow. Or they may sit and sulk. They show anger and fear by hissing. Rumbling growls are warning signs.

When they are not looking for food, polar bears often play. They splash and dunk each other. They box with their big paws. They do high dives and somersaults and slide down icy slopes. Their fur is slippery, so they don't even need sleds!

During the cold, arctic winter, it's hard for polar bears to find food. Sometimes the bears come onto the land to build dens. They lie down and dig a tunnel into the snow. They allow falling or blowing snow to cover the entrance. The bear's furry body and warm breath heat up the snowy nest.

Male polar bears usually stay in their dens only during December and January, the coldest months of the year. Female bears, however, spend most of the winter in their dens. In January, the females give birth to baby cubs. They usually have twins.

When the cubs are born, they are only as big as squirrels! They weigh just over a pound. The little bears cannot see or hear. The cubs' ears open about four weeks after birth. Their eyes open a week later.

By the time spring arrives, the cubs are about four months old. The mother knows when it is springtime because the air is warmer. She digs her way to the sunshine. Her cubs follow.

Polar bear cubs stay with their mothers for about two years. The mother teaches the cubs how to survive in the cold climate. She teaches them to hunt and swim. Mother polar bears also teach their cubs how to protect themselves. Although polar bears are one of the largest animals that live in the Arctic, they still have enemies. Musk-oxen, killer whales, and walruses can kill young polar bears.

Polar bears' worst enemies, however, are humans. Many people shoot polar bears for trophies. Hunters also kill them for their glossy white fur. Rugs, boots, coats, and warm mittens can be made from polar bear fur. Some people kill mother bears and sell their cubs to zoos and circuses.

The number of polar bears in the world is getting smaller because more and more people are killing them. Governments are now making laws against hunting these mighty animals. Hopefully, these laws will protect the remaining wild polar bears. They are beautiful animals that can never be replaced.